Some of the things you need
for this book

your head

a pencil

an eraser

magic

a pair
of scissors

a super-loud laugh

hahahaha!!!

(You'll have to think a little bit, too.)

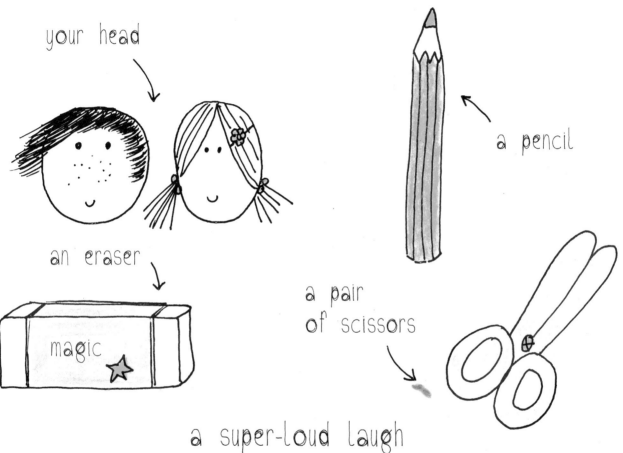

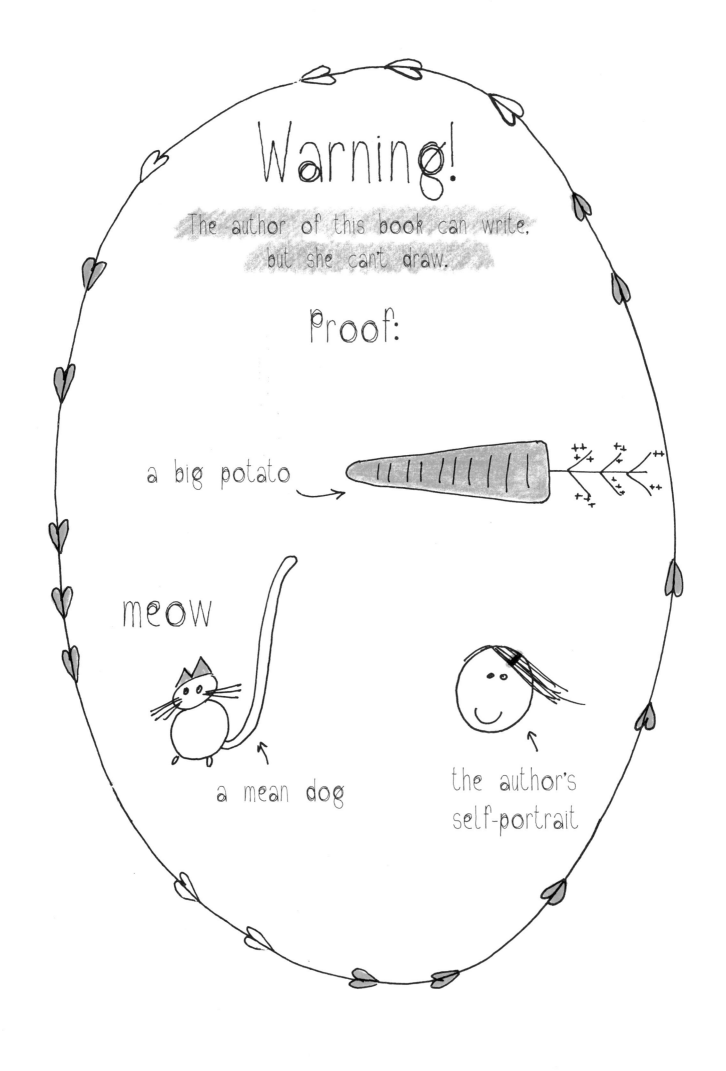

Are you ready to start this word adventure?

date: _ _ _ _ _ _ _ _ _ _ _

last name: _ _ _ _ _ _ _ _ _ _ _

first name: _ _ _ _ _ _ _ _ _

I am: ☐ a girl

☐ a boy

☐ a giant hamster

Sign here:

WHAT ARE WORDS FOR?

Check all that apply:

☐ to say what we think

☐ to write beautiful sentences

☐ to make ~~mestakes~~ mistakes during spelling tests

☐ to cook spaghetti

☐ to kid around with your friends

☐ to discuss things with your parents

☐ to make new friends

☐ to make prank phone calls (Don't do this!)

(next) ⟶

- ☐ to put feelings into words
- ☐ to give advice
- ☐ to explain what makes you sad
- ☐ to tell stories
- ☐ to sing songs
- ☐ to write love letters
- ☐ to comfort others
- ☐ to share your thoughts
- ☐ to write in your diary or journal

answer:

ALL OF THE ABOVE
(EXCEPT FOR COOKING SPAGHETTI)

✳ An Easy Game ✳

The letters of a very important word are out of order.

Put the letters back in order by connecting the dots with arrows:

1. →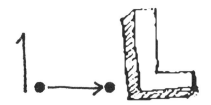

2.

3.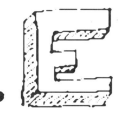

4.

answer: _ _ _ _

*A Page to Write Other
Very Important Words

* A Page of Magic Words

Check the magic words:

- ☐ thank you
- ☐ chocolate truffles
- ☐ vacuum cleaner
- ☐ please
- ☐ air
- ☐ love
- ☐ spider legs
- ☐ excuse me
- ☐ ravioli
- ☐ computer

What are your favorite magic words?

. . . .

. . . .

. . . .

Don't forget!!!...
Words can
have magical
powers!!!...

abracadabra©

Important!

→ Sometimes, words hurt:

→ Sometimes, words heal:

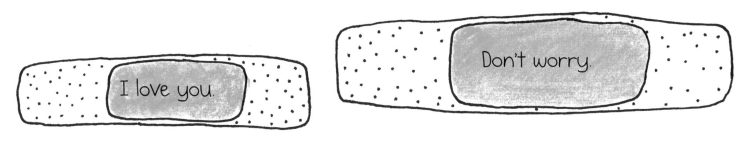

→ Always think before you use them!

BOX OF
24 WORD
BANDAGES

nobooboo©

* A Little Riddle *

What's the difference between:

A SWEAR WORD

and

an old pair of stinky socks?

X⚡☂↑ZZcrotte de...☹doui%6@ %❀@@@ZZ

answer:
_ _ _ _ _ _

There isn't any. They are both ugly and stinky and make people feel bad.

* A Funny T-shirt *

materials: 1 white t-shirt
1 fabric pen

Once upon a time...

Write a funny story on a t-shirt.
Put it on and wear it around all of your friends.

✳ Dream Page #1 ✳

✳

Describe your favorite dream
or the dream you had last night:

✳ Yum-Yum ✳

Decorate this cake with all
of your favorite words:

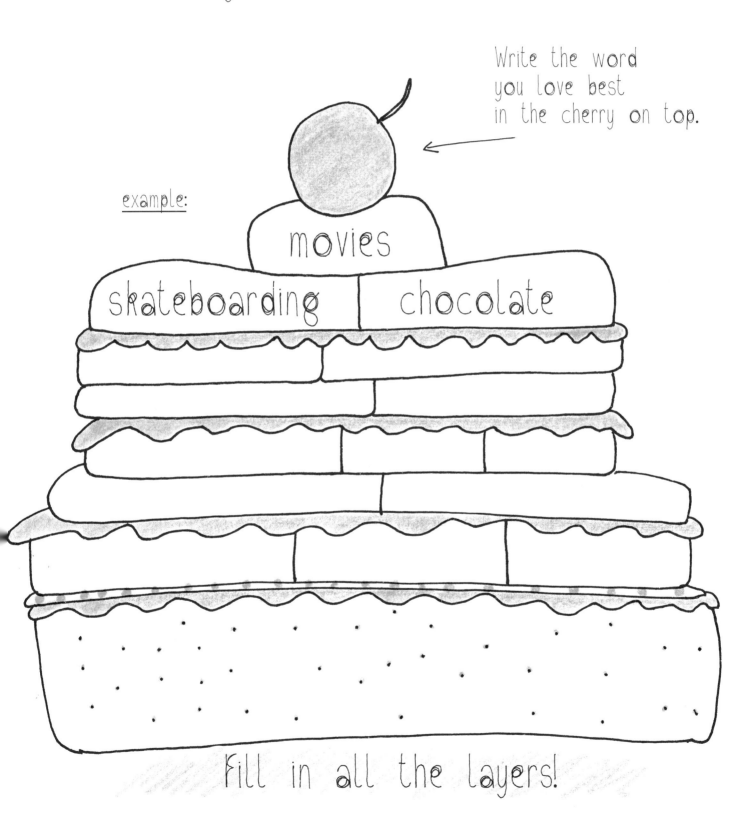

Write the word
you love best
in the cherry on top.

example:

movies

skateboarding   chocolate

Fill in all the layers!

* A Joke Letter to Your Parents *

How cool!

Instructions:

1) Cut out the letter. 2) Write your first name on the dotted line. 3) Ask your parents for an envelope and a stamp. 4) (Don't forget to change your handwriting on the envelope.)

Dear Sir or Madam:

I'm writing to remind you that your child, _____ , is totally **extraordinary** + unique + funny + magnificent and that you are extremely lucky to have him/her (even though his/her bedroom looks like it's exploded and he/she never listens to you).

Sincerely, A big fan of

_____

(the back
    of the letter)

*A Super-Simple Quiz for the Weekend *

GROUP A

silly television shows

pointless video games

soda

fast food

GROUP B

nature

friends

your favorite magazine

swimming

bicycle riding

roller blading

→ Guess which group is the healthiest?

(Hint: it starts with the letter "b.")

Write your answer here.

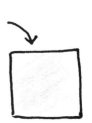

* A Little Group of Words that Make Your Eyes Water *

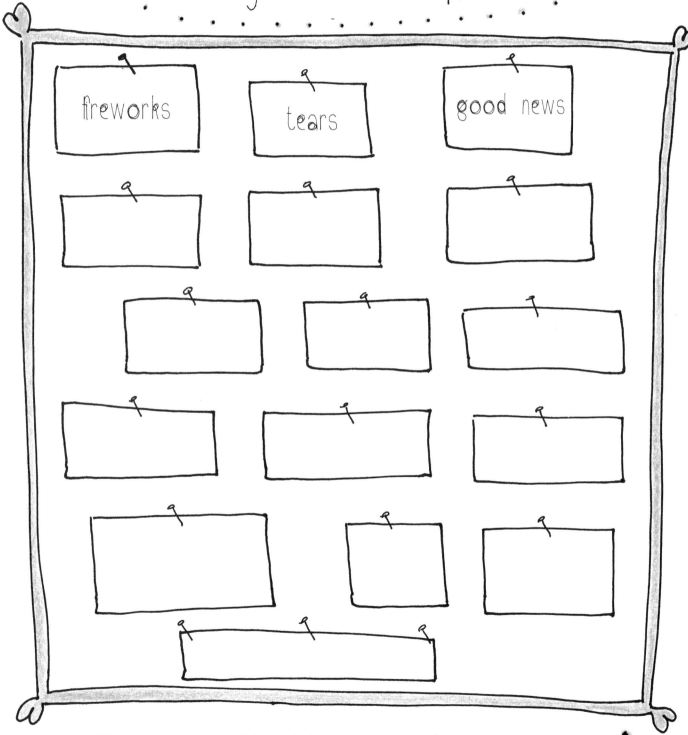

fireworks

tears

good news

Fill in all the empty spaces. ↑

*A Little Group of Words that Make You Laugh

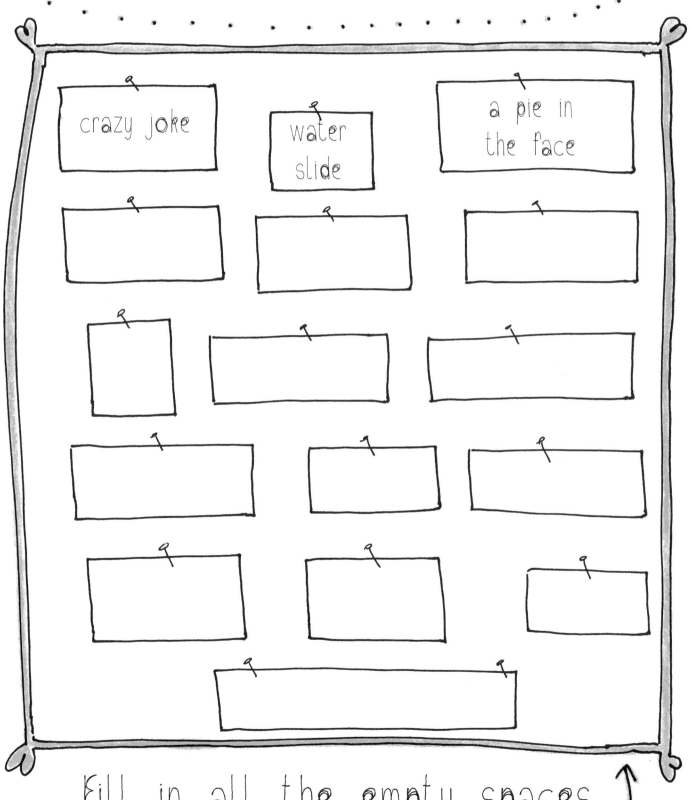

crazy joke

water slide

a pie in the face

Fill in all the empty spaces.

A Super-Spelling Super Hero...

special memory mask

super glasses to see and focus better

cape to hide answers from others

flying underwear to get him to the library faster

What is Super-
Spelling Man's
secret?

I read a lot !!!

Do what he does!

✳ Write a Poem ✳

♥ ♥ ♥ ♥ ♥ ♥ ♥ ♥ ♥ ♥ ♥ ♥

Write a poem with ten lines, and make each line end with a rhyme:

1 . . . .

2 . . . .

3 . . . .

4 . . . .

5 . . . .

6 . . . .

7 . . . .

8 . . . .

9 . . . .

10 . . . .

✳ <u>A rhyming tip</u>: don't try and rhyme the word "centipede."

Write your poem on scratch paper first!

More Poetry

✱   ✱

Different lines of a poem can contain different numbers of syllables. Count the syllables in each line of this poem and put the number in the box. (Sometimes it helps if you clap and count.)

number of syllables:

The Centipede's Dilemma !

A centipede has   — — — — — — — — → example: → **5**

One hundred feet.

They're not all clean

And they're not all neat.

The hardest thing

Is shopping for shoes,

He likes lots of styles

And he never can choose.

(author anonymous)

> I just couldn't decide which shoes to wear!

barefoot centipede
↓

* A Page to Write the Words You Think Are Really Weird or Really Funny

ex.: waffle
    squiggle

* A Postcard to Mail to Yourself When You Need a Laugh

(or when you're feeling sad)

1) Cut out the postcard. 2) On the back, write lots of compliments about yourself. 3) If you want, put it in an envelope so it doesn't get damaged. 4) Write your address on the envelope. 5) Borrow a stamp, and mail it!

(the back of the postcard to fill
out using your best handwriting)

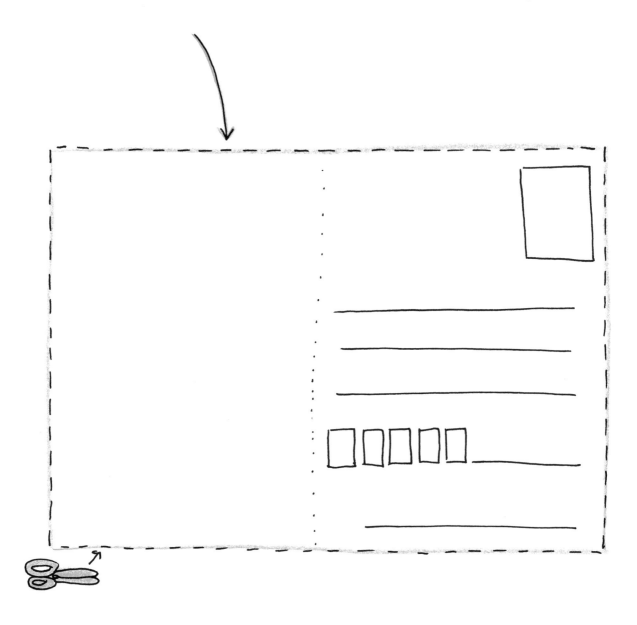

You'll be so happy when
this arrives in your mailbox!

✳ The Smallest Bookstore
in the World!

♡♡♡♡ ♡♡ ♡ ♡♡♡♡

1 Cut it out (cut along the thick black lines).

2 Fold along the dotted lines.

3 Apply glue to the sections marked with diagonal lines, stick together and assemble!
(If you're little, ask for help so you don't mess up.)

Here it is!

(the back of the world's
smallest bookstore)

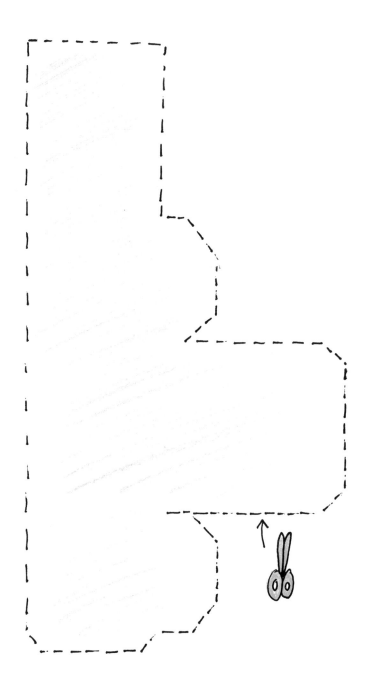

Pretend your best friend has broken their foot. Write lots of nice things on their cast.

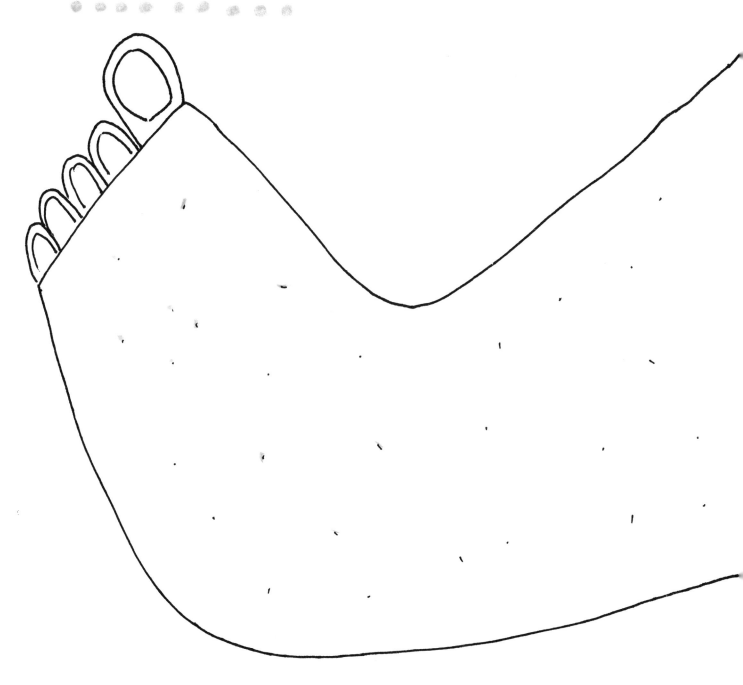

Create a whispering pillow
to help you get a good
night's sleep.

This pillow protects
me from monsters
and nightmares

reallysoft©

Use a fabric pen to write
on the pillowcase.

✳ Dream Page #2 ✳

Describe your funniest or happiest dream:

Repeat this sentence 5 times fast.

"I must put the cap back on my marker, otherwise it will dry out like a gazelle dying of thirst in a desert and the vultures will eat it."

Proof:

← the skeleton of a dead marker (no cap)

* A Blank Page *

Write whatever you want.

✳ A Funny Saying ✳

Sometimes, you have to eat your words!

serving size, one person!

AN EMBARRASSING BUT DELICIOUS STORY TO GULP DOWN

100 pages

✳ Do you know what this saying means?

✳ Have you ever felt like that?

✳ When? . . . .
. . . .

answer:

Don't worry! It happens to everyone.

* What are you thinking?
Write it down inside the bubble!

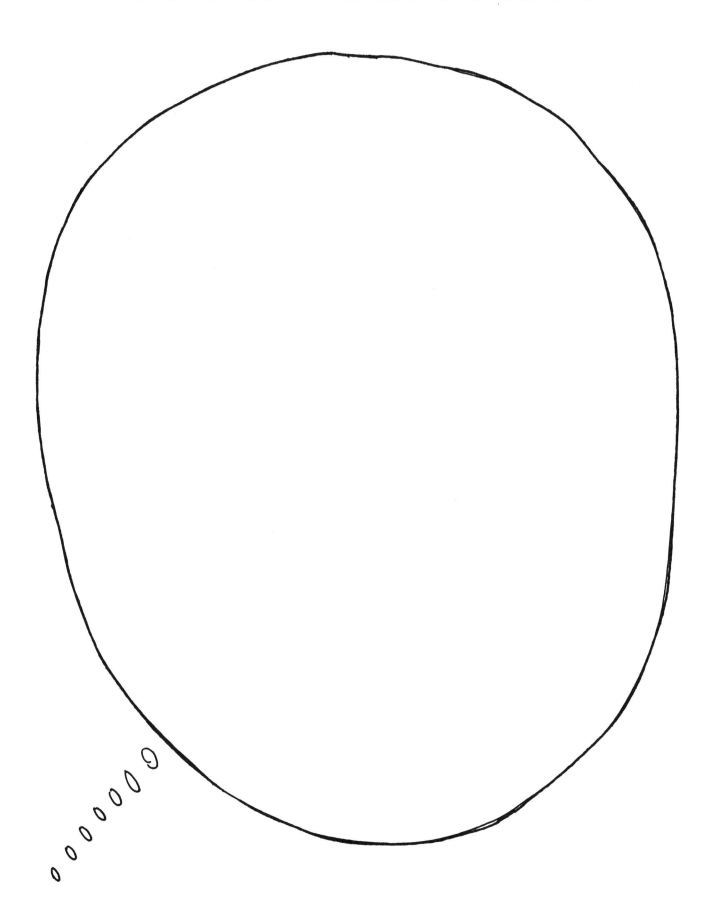

Bathtub
Baby
Banana
Basket
Bingo

Repeat these words as fast
as you can 10 times - without laughing!

✳ The Word Box ✳

1. Find a shoe box to decorate.

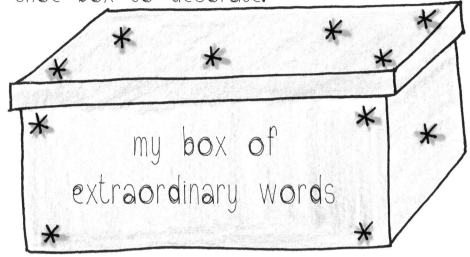

my box of
extraordinary words

2. Cut out beautiful, bizarre or funny words from magazines.

3. Close your eyes and pick some of the words you've cut out, then arrange them into sentences and decorate your box!

example:

Oh moon, give me a yummy, shining piece of toast.

Now, go play with your friends!

*A Weightless Word Mobile

Choose words from this list that sound or seem light and airy, then use them to fill in the mobile on the next page.

list:

yahoo!
birthday
tears
joke
nightmare
accident
friend
homework
whipped cream
fight
truck
feather
gift
laughter
petal
nice!

bubble
wind
rain
storm
dream
sky
flower
candle
cloud
bird
dinosaur
stone
giggle
gumdrop
grass
lazy!

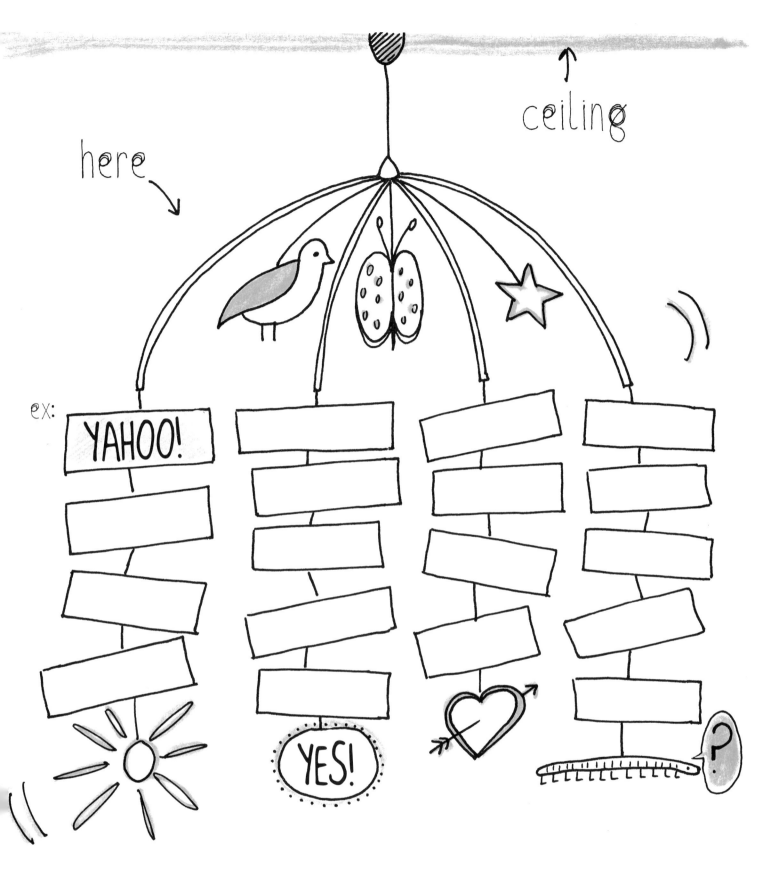

Careful: if you put heavy words
on the mobile it will fall!

* Some Good

① Always leave a stack of books next to your bed.

② Ask your friends what their favorite books are and trade with them.

Book Advice

③ Always bring a book with you
when you know you'll have to wait.

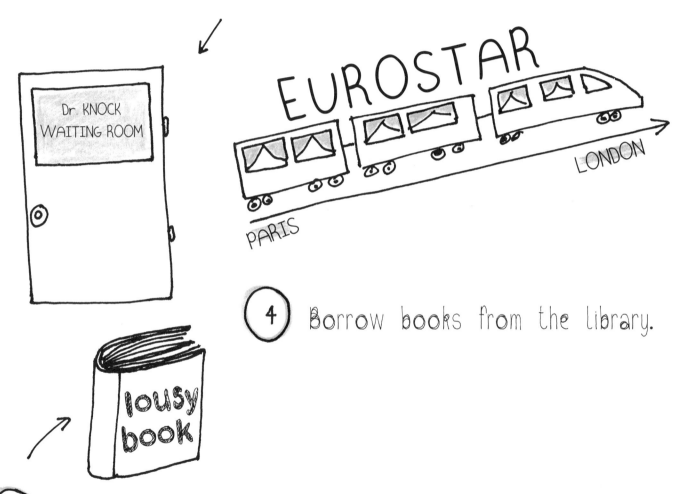

Dr. KNOCK
WAITING ROOM

EUROSTAR

PARIS

LONDON

④ Borrow books from the library.

lousy
book

⑤ If you don't like a book you don't have
to finish it, but always start another one!

* The Page for Making Up and Practicing
# New Signatures

Close this
book.
Put it on your
head and spin
around while
you say the
alphabet three
times.
Don't let the
book fall off!

* Creating Characters with Letters of the Alphabet

examples:

Miss Adorable

Wonderful Wilma

Peter Moustache

Now it's your turn!
Create characters, and don't
forget to make up names
for them too.

R

i

o

t

· · · · · · · · · · · ·

· · · · · · · · · · ·

· · · · · · · · · · ·

· · · · · · · · · · · ·

S.O.S. Words

1

Caution!!! Try not to make too many spelling mistakes. It hurts the words and then they have to go to the hospital...

. . . and to get back at you, the words will call your teacher and tell her to give you an "F" in spelling.

* Write the words
that really make you mad
in capital letters.   *

at home

ex.: **GOING TO BED EARLY**

at school

A Page to Cut Out and Stick Up in Your Room

I ♥ Reading

(the back of the page
to cut out and stick up
in your room)

Make a Bookmark!

1

Cut a rectangle out of white cardboard.

2

Punch a hole in one corner and thread a piece of yarn through it (tie a knot in the end).

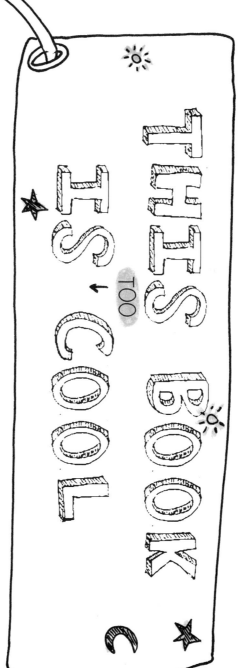

THIS BOOK IS TOO COOL

3

Write something funny on the cardboard.

4

Decorate with glitter.

✳ A Find-the-Mistake Game ✳

Find the spelling mistakes on these packages, then correct them.

chocolate

100 % mold

Pure Cactus

↑

The more you eat,
the worse you feel.

power
sugar

It's Electrifying!

↑

It will light up
your life.

100 %
pure
foot juice

Freshly
Squeezed

sounds delicious

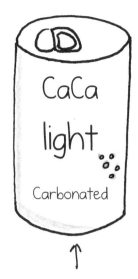

CaCa
light

Carbonated

100% No thanks!

extra
crazy butter

for extra crazy buttered toast?

BIO

Bio yogross
natural

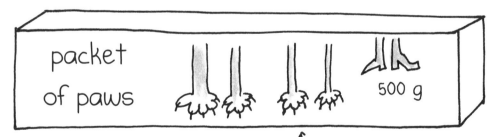

packet
of paws

500 g

They make drinking
a little hairy.

24 pretzel licks

crispy and delicious

Yum! Not!

* Hold this page up
to a mirror:

*

✱ You can learn how to write in reversed letters too!

(1) Take a piece of white paper and use a black marker to write whatever you want on it.

(2) Turn the paper over and, using your marker, trace the backwards writing that shows through. (You can also tape the paper to a window to help you see through it better.)

Write your first name in reversed letters and stick it here:

*Special Double-Page Spread of Swear Words

a Ask your parents for three swear words that you have permission to use when you need them:

1
2
3

Remember: they can't be real and they have
to be funny.
(example: stinking bird pooh-pooh!)

b Invent some more!

Words and Ideas

Sometimes one word will spark another, or even a whole bunch. For example:

If you hear...	What do you think of?
ocean	
Sunday	
sky	
vacation	
nighttime	
toe	

(Don't think about it too much, just write whatever comes into your head.)

* A Silly Idea for Bathroom Humor *

1 Take the toilet paper from the bathroom.
2 Carefully unroll about 3 feet.
3 Leave the first 4 squares blank and on the next squares, write messages
   or jokes using a fine-tip marker (put a magazine underneath the squares
   so you don't have to press down too hard).
4 Re-roll the paper like nothing ever happened.
5 Put it back where it belongs.

so funny!

↑
joke-scented toilet paper

Some examples
of love letters
with no spelling
mistakes to copy
if you need them

To a boy

Dear . . . . (write his first name)

I've been thinking of you every 3 to 5 minutes
since the first time I saw you eating fries
in the cafeteria.
I think you're super good-looking and super funny.
All my friends think you're really good-looking too
so that's why I'm rushing to write to you first!
I would like it a lot if you wanted to be friends.
So here's the secret code: If you want to be friends,
wear your red t-shirt with the motorcycle
on it tomorrow, or else you can wear whatever you
want, I don't care.
(By the way, I don't ski on the bunny slopes anymore!)

Signed . . . . (your first name)

To a girl

Dear . . . . (write her first name)

I really, really, really like you and when I see you,
my heart beats like this: badaboom badaboom badaboom.
Can you hear it?
I've written some poems in my head for you.
I think about you all the time.
When I grow up, I'm going to travel to the moon.
Do you want to come?
If you do, meet me behind the wall of the cafeteria during the
next recess.

Signed . . . . (your first name)

✳ Certain things are hard to say, so sometimes it's easier if you write them down.

example:

Dear Parents,

Yes, I admit: I was the one that broke the window and put the worm in the pasta.

I'm sorry.

Slip this little note
under your parents' bedroom door!

Making Your Own
Magic Words

examples

abracadabracasiskoombabra!
abracadabrasupersabra!

Now it's your turn:

* abracadabra _ _ _ _ _ _ _ _ _ _ _

_ _ _ _ _ _ _ _ _ _ _ _ _ _ _ _ _ _ _ _

(Close your eyes, place both hands on your head and repeat your magic word three times.)

* The Imagination Page *

Describe the life you want
to have when you grow up.

* Sometimes words have hidden meanings.

For example, if your mom says:

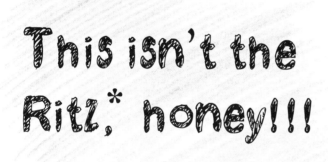

This isn't the Ritz,* honey!!!

*(The Ritz is a 5-star hotel.)

She means:

1) You should clear the table after every meal.

2) There's no room service in this house.

3) No one is going to put away your roller blades for you.

Super-Cool
Secret Passwords
for Your Next Mission:

*Connect the warm words to the oven and the cold words to the refrigerator.

kiss •

hug •

celebrate •

scar •

macaroni and cheese •

flame •

grudge •————————————→ •

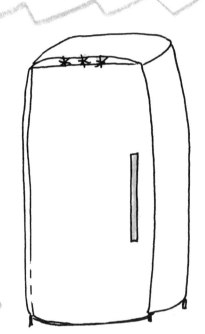

sunburn •

bad news •

birthday party •

blanket •

•

ice cream •

hair •

compliment •

radiator •

insult •

What's the difference?

* Secrets *

Use it to record all of your adventures!

* A Memory that
Warms Your Heart...

* Write your first book!

(It's easy!)

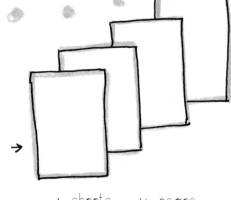

1 Take a few pieces of blank white paper.

4 sheets = 16 pages

2 Put them on top of each other in a neat pile.

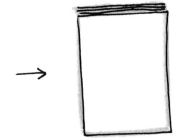

3 Fold the pile of papers in half and press firmly along the fold.

4 Punch two holes near the top and bottom of the fold and thread a ribbon through them, then tie a knot in the ribbon.

5 Write the title of your book and decorate the cover.

6 Next, write down a story or some poems - don't forget to illustrate them!

Make more copies to give away!

✱ Make your own envelopes!

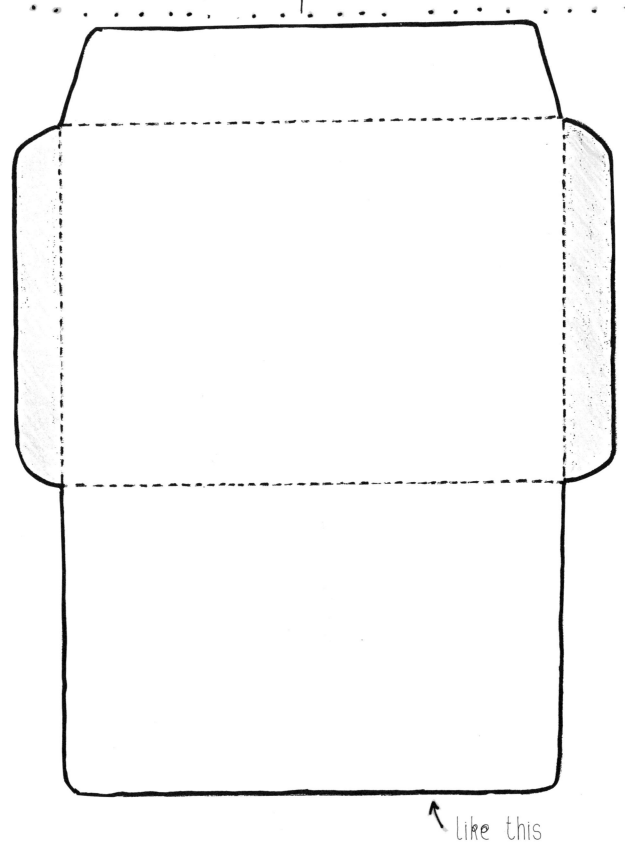

↖ like this

How to Do It

1) Trace the sample on the opposite page onto a piece of paper and then cut out the pattern.

2) Fold on the dotted lines.

3) Put glue on the shaded parts.

4) Glue down the flaps.

Decorate your envelope
or make it out
of homemade paper!

Fill this page with
the hardest words you know:

* Silly Things We Say *

Sometimes, words escape me.

FEROCIOUS WORDS

DANGER!

You think you're so smart!

grrr
grroarrr

I hate you!

* Are those good things to say?

* Do you say those things sometimes?

* When? . . . .

. . . .

answers:

1) It's hard not to say things when you're angry, but you should try to be careful. Words can be dangerous.

2) Sometimes we can't find the right words when we need them. Maybe it's better not to say anything when that happens?

Yum!!
Let's make talking cookies!

Hide notes, jokes, riddles or fortunes inside these cookies. They're great for parties.

I love you, Grandma!

You will have a long and happy life.

Merry Christmas!

What did the shoe say to the sock?

BOX OF TALKING COOKIES

Give them away!

Invite your friends to read and eat.

The Recipe

Ingredients (makes 15 cookies): 3 egg whites + 1 cup flour + 3/4 cup sugar + 1/2 cup butter + 1/4 teaspoon vanilla + pinch of salt + 1 colored marker + colored paper (it's prettier) + 1 small spoon to flatten the cookie dough .

----) Preheat the oven to 375 degrees.

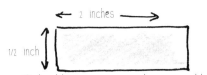

1) Cut the paper into small strips.

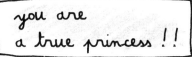

2) Write a message on each strip and fold the strips in half.

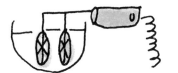

3) Beat the egg whites, the salt and the sugar until frothy.

4) Melt the butter, then let it cool.

5) Mix the butter, flour and vanilla in a large mixing bowl.

egg whites

6) Fold in the egg white & sugar mixture.

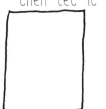

7) Grease a cookie sheet.

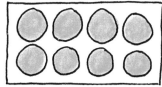

8) Spoon the dough into 2-inch circles on the cookie sheet making sure the dough has room to spread. (Use the spoon to spread the dough into circles.)

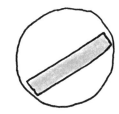

9) Put the cookies in the oven and bake for 5 minutes at 375 degrees. Remove the cookies as soon as the edges are golden brown.

10) Working quickly, put one of the folded messages on top of each cookie.

11) Carefully fold each cookie in half like a half moon, pressing down on the edges only, not the middle.

Be quick! Don't let the cookie dough set!

12) Put the cookies on a plate to cool.

Warning! Always tell people that a message is hidden inside!

*

Finish this story
(give it <u>a happy ending</u>).

· ·

Once upon a time there was a blue elephant
who was dying of hunger...

Hooray! version

Finish this story
(give it <u>a sad ending</u>).

Once upon a time there was a pink elephant who was dying of hunger...

Boo-Hoo! version

✳ Inventing Imaginary Words

(Use the beginning of one word and the end of another.)

example: a teachraffe

a teacher with a long neck and a giraffe's head that can see everything going on in the back of the classroom

1 yard

Hey! Back there. Have you finished goofing off?

✻ # Your Turn

Make up the word:

_____

What does it mean?

_____

Draw it:

_____

Impress your parents!!!
Learn to speak French!!!

Sentences with really hard to pronounce French words:	Say them like this:
J'aimerais plus d'argent de poche, s'il vous plait	Juh aimeray ploose de rjant duh posh, see vah plate?

→ In English, you would say: I would love more allowance, please.

Ces nouvelles chaussures sont trop mignonnes! Pourriez-vous me les offrir, s'il vous plait?	Say newvel showsure sont tro minyons! Pouray-voo muh lays offrear, see vah plate?

→ In English, you would say: Those new shoes are so cute! May I have them, please?

Practice until it hurts!!!

List all the foreign words you know:

* A good idea: Word Confetti!

1) Take a piece of white paper and cut it into lots of small pieces.

2) Write something on each piece (something you've always wanted, for example).

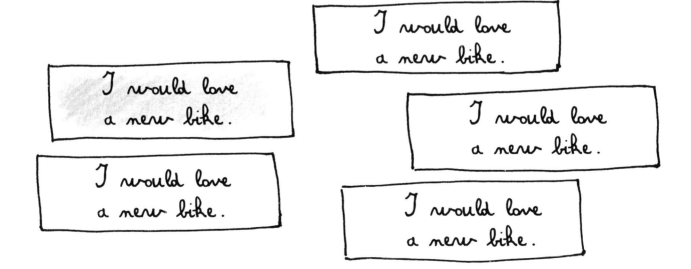

3) Put the pieces of paper in a beautiful box. →

DREAM
cat dog bike

4) Ask your dad or mom to sit down and close their eyes.

5) Dump the contents of the box on their head while saying:

abracadabra!

It might work!

You can do the same thing for birthdays, but instead of what you want, write something nice about the birthday person.

You are the best dad in the world !

You are the best mom in the world !

*What do these sounds

Connect the dots from one page to the other:

bwaaaa haaaa haaaaa haaaa *

chomp crunch chomp crunch chomp *

tsk tsk tsk tsk * —— example

pssssst pssssssst *

kiss kiss kiss kiss *

woooohooo   woooohooo *

slurp dribble slurp dribble *

aha! aha! aha! *

make you think of? ✳

* the sound your dad makes when he's not happy
  (and you're not happy either)

* the sounds people make when they're head-over-
  heels about someone

* the sound your friend makes when you tell
  a really good joke

* the sound you make when you remember something
  you thought you'd forgotten

* the sound you make when you sneak a box
  of cookies and gobble them up

* the sound you make when you pass a note
  to a friend

* the sound of the last day of school

* the sound of ice cream on a hot day

* Compare these two pages.

drawing (a)

a pencil that has never been sharpened

Ahhhhhhh!
I'm useless!!
I'm not good for anything!!!!
I feel terrible!

never-been-used end

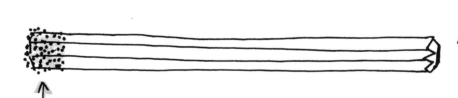

brand-new eraser

<u>poor</u>, <u>poor</u>
<u>pencil</u>

Which drawing is the saddest?

drawing (b)

a perfectly sharpened pencil

magnificent point

perfect end

Woo Hoo!!!
I feel great!
Here come the
good grades
and fantastic
drawings!

Write your answer here.

* Things that
Scare You:

* Advice for a Friend *

If you say:

> "Hand me that <u>thing</u> that's next to the <u>whatchamacallit</u>."

We might hear:

1) Hand me the dog next to the couch.

2) Hand me the sausage next to the television.

3) Hand me the underpants next to the mushroom.

4) Anything else!

---> Use words carefully and precisely if you want to be understood!

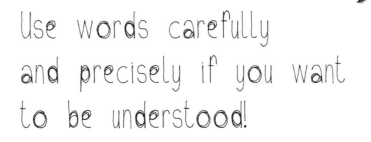

* The "Shhhhhhhh" Page *

Stop!

CLOSE YOUR EYES FOR JUST A MINUTE AND ENJOY THE QUIET!

* Describe what you heard:

_ _ _ _ _ _ _ _ _ _ _ _ _

_ _ _ _ _ _ _ _ _ _ _ _

_ _ _ _ _ _ _ _ _ _ _

* Do you like the sounds of silence?

_ _ _ _ _ _ _ _ _ _ _ _

_ _ _ _ _ _ _ _ _ _ _

Dancing
the Word Hip-Hop!

Write down your favorite poem and
then make up a funny dance to do while you
recite it. Teach your friends!

You can roll on the floor and spin around
and change words to make it even funnier!

You should never be too afraid to enter the dictionary!
It's the words' house - almost all of them live here!

The dictionary's job is to help you understand... everything!

* How does it work?

1. To find where a word lives and what it means, first you open the door of the dictionary building.

2. Next, find the floor with the first letter of the word.

3. Once you find the right floor, go down the hall and read the words on the doors until you come to your word.
For example, on the T floor you'll find:

target   tariff   tarmac   tarn   tarnish

4. Open the door of the word you want to find and then you can read its definition.
(ex.: tarn = a small mountain lake)

See? It's easy!

*** Write 3 words that ***
start with each letter!

a   example: audio   applaud   apple

b

c

d

e

f

g

h

i

j

k

l
m
n
o
p
k
r
s
t
u
v
W
x
y
Z

Now it's getting complicated!

Okay, you're allowed to go

to bed instead.

zzzzzzz....

A Letter to Santa Claus

Or, why you should always be very careful when you're writing something important!

\- - - - - - - - - - ->

letter a

Dear Santa,

This letter is to tell you what
I'd really like for Christmas:
a new pair of basketball shoes
gold earrings
an orange guitar
a trip to the circus
I'd really like a cd player for
my room if that's not too much.
and I wish I could have a ride
on your reindeer.

Thanks in advance,

letter b

Dear Sunta,

This leter is to sell you whut I'd
rily like for Chrissmas:

a new pear of basketball shows
gold hearings
an orange getar
a trip to the serkus
I'd rily like a cd plaer for my
room if that's not two much,
and I wish I culd have a rid on
your rainder.

→ the 25ᵗʰ of December...

Noël

game

orange

* Cross off the line that doesn't rhyme.

* It really won't surprise,
* To hear that I don't like flies.
* And you don't have to be wise,
* To guess that I love french fries,
* Whatever the size.
* You might surmise,
* By this,
* That while I don't tell lies,
* And though I like to advise,
* I'm not always wise.
* Particularly about the fries' size.
* Because eating too many is hardly wise,
* But better than eating flies.
* That I can advise,
* And it should come as no surprise.

*

* Describe the most amazing day of your life: *

* What's a lame excuse?

examples:

I didn't clear the table last night because I had to catch a flight to France.

I didn't clean up my room because I was on the phone with the President.

I didn't finish my homework because my hamster was a little depressed and I had to stay up late and talk to him all night long.

→ Write your own!

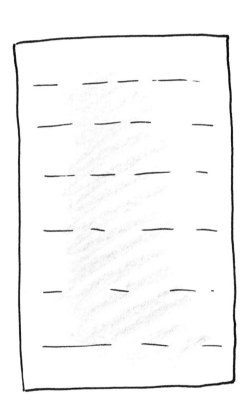

List all the words
you really don't like:

-
-
-
-
-
-
-
-
-
-
-

✳ The One-Minute, One-Letter Game ✳

1 Close your eyes and let the point of your pencil land wherever it wants on any page of this book.

2 Open your eyes and find out what letter your pencil point landed on.

3 You have one minute to come up with as many words as you can that begin with this letter. (Your friends can play too.)

For example, if you landed on the letter :

alphabet   ape

amazing   airplane

antelope   annoy

automobile   advice

* Secret Code

Rules: replace each letter with a number between 1-26 as shown in the chart below:

a	b	c	d	e	f	g	h	i	j	k	l	m	n
=	=	=	=	=	=	=	=	=	=	=	=	=	=
1	2	3	4	5	6	7	8	9	10	11	12	13	14

o	p	q	r	s	t	u	v	w	x	y	z
=	=	=	=	=	=	=	=	=	=	=	=
15	16	17	18	19	20	21	22	23	24	25	26

What does this say?

20 | 8 | 9 | 19   9 | 19   20 | 8 | 5   2 | 5 | 19 | 20

___ ___ ___ ___ ___ ___ ___ ___ ___ ___ ___ ___ ___

2 | 15 | 15 | 11   5 | 22 | 5 | 18 | !

___ ___ ___ ___ ___ ___ ___ ___   (Write the letter on the line under the number.)

Now, write your best friend's name using the code chart:

(Don't forget the spaces between the words!)

first name: _ _ _ _ _ _ _ _ _ _ _ _

last name: _ _ _ _ _ _ _ _ _ _ _ _

a little friendly advice

Write with a pencil and erase quickly if you spot a spy (or if you plan on changing best friends anytime soon)!

* That's Life! Don't Worry! *

Sometimes, words pour down on you like rain.

Marvelous and fabulous!
My sweetheart, my honey bun, my teddy bear
Come here so I can give you a huggggggg!!!!!!!!!!!!!!!!!
I adore you!
Too handsome, too EVERYTHING!
My princess!
Super-spectacular!
I LOVE YOU!
You're simply magical, my dear.
My superhero!
You're too cool, too funny, too smart, too nice.

how could you ruin another pair of jeans
you are a slob
you exaggerate
you are rude and not funny at all
where is your backpack
your room is a mess
you're getting on my nerves
you'll be sorry
you are bugging me
you do whatever you want and you don't think
I don't believe you
you are a bad friend

a big warm rain
of compliments

a small cold rain
of reproaches

drip drop drip drop drip....

✳ Another Funny Expression ✳

Sometimes, feeling tired, upset, shy
or emotional will leave you "speechless."

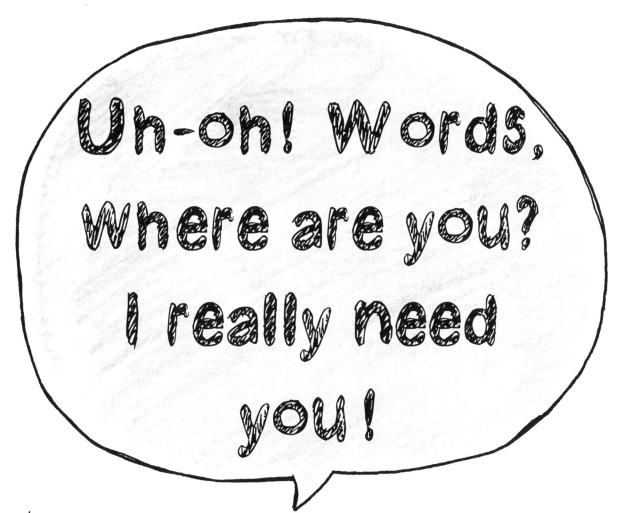

Uh-oh! Words, where are you? I really need you!

✳ Do you know what this means?
✳ Does it happen to you sometimes?
✳ When? . . . .
. . . .
answer: . . . .

It means we don't know what to say, so we don't say anything at all.

* Write down 3 jobs you might like to have when you grow up, and why you'd like to have them.

job #1	why?
job #2	why?
job #3	why?

*Fill in the letters! You need these words to take photos:

ch _ _ _ e!

_ m _ _ e!

These words make better pictures.
Try it and you'll see!

answers:

Cheese! Smile!

* List Your Favorite Books *

#1

#2

#3

#4

#5

#6

#7

#8

#9

#10

(Warning!!! If you don't list *I Love Words* as one of your favorite books your school will be struck by lightning and you'll get chicken pox.)

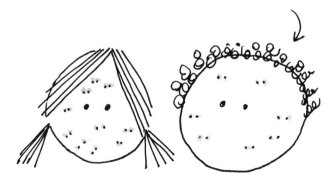

✳ Challenge #1 ✳

Make up a short story using these 3 words:
bubblegum + cloud + sidewalk

✳ Challenge #2 ✳

Make up a short story that
ends with "So he bought
a parrot who spoke Japanese."

✳ Challenge #3 ✳

Make up a short story that
takes place on the moon
in the year 3000...

* Complete this page if you are sick of words!

Draw your best friends and don't write their names.

This is where you write the words that you usually find on the last page of a book or the end of a story:

___ ___ ___

___ ___ ___

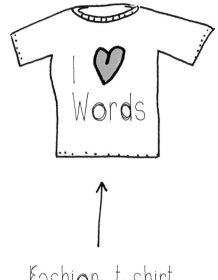

fashion t-shirt
(It's in the book.)

To Lou, Gabin, Clémentine and Chloé

First American Edition 2010
Kane Miller, A Division of EDC Publishing

First published in France in 2009 under the title *J'aime les mots* by hélium,
12, rue de l'Arbalète - 75005 Paris
Copyright © hélium

Library of Congress Control Number: 2009932397

Manufactured by Regent Publishing Services, Hong Kong
Printed February 2012 in ShenZhen, Guangdong, China
3 4 5 6 7 8 9 10

ISBN: 978-1-935279-48-8